KT-471-727

Herefordshire
Council

NHS
Herefordshire

Working in partnership for the people of Herefordshire

BEE JOURNAL

BEE JOURNAL

Sean Borodale

CAPE POETRY

Published by Jonathan Cape 2012

2 4 6 8 10 9 7 5 3 1

Addresse   an be found at:

ISBN 9780224097215

The Random House Group Limited supports The Forest Stewardship Council
(FSC®), the leading international forest certification organisation. Our books
carrying the FSC label are printed on FSC® certified paper. FSC is the only
forest certification scheme endorsed by the leading environmental organisations,
including Greenpeace. Our paper procurement policy can be found at
www.randomhouse.co.uk/environment

Typeset by Palimpsest Book Production Limited, Falkirk, Stirlingshire

Printed and bound in Great Britain by
MPG Books Ltd, Bodmin, Cornwall

for Jane, Orlando and Louis

*Economists understand about work about as much
as alchemists about gold.*
                    Ivan Illich, 'Shadow Work'

BEE JOURNAL

24TH MAY: COLLECTING THE BEES

I'd say it's toiling air, high up here;
steep with bees, and the beacon sun
burns
overlapping light, close to sundown.

Come to collect bees, our hive in parts.
Compound of fencing, stands of nucleus hives.
(Nuc,
new word.)

He just wears a veil, this farmer, no gloves
and lifts open a dribbly wax-clogged
blackwood box.
We in our whites mute with held breath.
Hello bees.
Drops four frames into our silence.

The air is like mica
ancient with thin flecks;
distance viewed through a filter of thousands.
I am observed.

Each box has the pulsar of its source. Porous with eyes
we wait in the spinning sun. The light is Medusa,
sugar of frayed threads; a mesh, a warp-field, all
the skin of our heads.

24TH MAY: HOME

Forty miles west of here
a farmer was lifting, turning frames
in gloveless hands
from his box into ours.

Our hive now holds her bees,
night falls.

It sat behind us in the small red car;
noise inescapable.
Were we to crash it would be catastrophic.
Think! Do not think.

The noise of weight;
we carried this
through our proscenium of grasses
to the stand we'd built.

It is alive; unknown components we have:
small, small, small sounds composing one.

Untaped their door; two staggered out,
they fell
onto the landing board; first deaths.

Other broken bodies limped
not travel sick, but
ejected into a province of forget.

Please, no ill omen tonight.

Well-banded in our torchlight,
the bees all blackened to a clutch, a clot:
she must be there.

We stepped back in the air.
Petals, stamens, anthers of flower sex;
nectar will bribe these bees.

Lifted on thought I flew briefly. Human dance.

Gloves, gauzes, white suits slumped –
I live in here.
That strange squat Jack-in-the-Box
seems prominent – *out there.*

27TH MAY: GEOGRAPHY

Bees in the roof, bees on the walls
stitching the house in a net of flightways,
just like surveillance, just like snoopers
in the open air.

And they rig crack, lump, recess, ridge
to the commune of a memory;
and they rig it
to the thin low wide little door
of the North in the hive over there;

and they rig it
to our conversation and commentary,
and the brittle sweat's armada of frightened water
on our brows;

and they rig it, finally, to the minutes
of the sun's last floodlit bit of daylight.

I had to say, today, I said,
you have us locked inside your noise-truss.

You are a brain in impermanence,
coding, knowing, keeping
the latitude and longitude of this, our house;
each bee a synapse slowly forming an arrival.

And in your trance I had to say, this is
an afternoon of lifetimes tightened into knots.

You have gradated us:
vibrations, colours, trajectories of substance,
and the thermals
turning this house to align with yours.

28TH MAY

The heavy brood frame
reeks with bees.
Still I have not seen
the queen's length, shape.

Amaze me, elusive maker of eggs,
your larvae catching light are lit
like life very young is lit
to see-through.

Your hive is a thought
all otherwise quiet;
a shape in a swaddling of noise
being sifted through;

each wing touch, leg rub, dance,
the air's big mass of flickers condensed.

Stop. *You, bee-friend,*
lifting a frame up to the light.
Sound of clicking, face peers close.
This is very sincere activity; we will be stung.

Various glow-blobs, dimmings of work,
living small bulbs of eye: note, bee glow.

29TH MAY: FEEDING SUGAR

I have the syrup feeder, its lidded reservoir
in both my hands,
going up to the hive for the third time ever.

Liquid I boiled and stirred the sugar into:
clear refined British beet.
It went, like magic does.

The plastic tub has an uncanny shifting weight.
I am their farmer.
I will for weeks give this, my gift.

Lifting the heavy brood frame weeping with bees
we are wax, translucent-feeling;
the weight already promises.

Being apiarists, we exploit this trust:
they let in our nerves.

They are impervious with process:
work-ethic tendency.
They do not pause
but play on in autoloop, and have phases.

We are in.

Jewellery box: I did not expect this strange calmness.
Eyes go steady with study of larvae,
womb, light, wax, bee eggs.

Still I have not seen the fountain of all,
where is *she*?
Must learn to find this instrument by heart.

One gold halo in a white room.

Neighbours-in-making, unlegged, unwinged.
No need for anything but mouth and anus now.
Will find flight.

This is a brain itself: congestion of language,
olfactory archive, register
of homeopathic light stored in amphorae.

You, bee man, lifting a frame to light, count only numbers.
You *are* human; what bees count must be more than parts.
Breathe on them your dream of honey-smeared taste.

They agitate and are in dream what sun pens.
Motherboard of many; each light, residual:
element, lumen, diode, valve.

This snapshot is vital; I take but cannot make.

I capture nothing – several drones are present.
Take note, they will be killed; should *I* take note?

5TH JUNE: BEE SMOKER

We went white-clothed from head to toe
with smoker:
Tin can with spout and bellow.

Smokery for bee visits,
each time hung up like fish or ham,
preserved.

They are transparent panes
when cut into;
their luminous glass flesh of times.

Few twigs and screws of paper
lit, smoke puffs and withers.

It makes a tenuous strange mark,
this mode of dissipation.

Note, if tapped the hive will roar;
did this; it did.
The battery test has worked,
some bumped the gauze.
Alive deranged edges of choked fire tapered.

This National hive is not a nation; its cedar box
was opened, saw their work like grains of rice.
My eye did not invent this?

Uncertain now, I must believe
I *did* count the tiny specks inside brood food.
Smoke veiled the scent of my amazement.

Brood food – I like that secret.
Secreted from the workers' heads
is royal jelly. That makes a queen.

Rain fell, smoke language drifted unsaid.
Will not use the smoke again, it seems unkind.

6TH JUNE: SUMMER NOTES

Today is anxiety.
No presence of the queen, maker of bodies.

Today is anxiety.
Not a length, not a gap between the working.

Today is anxiety.
Her own name frail as vapour just rubs off the tongue
wrong.

Who, if I call her,
who if I call in to the crawling tenements of workshop?
What should I call her? *New, central, unlit, a unit?*

Gauze, visor again, veil,
the white suit, until I, anonymous.

This is the beekeeper; generic, utility,
a slogan to be worn;
all-white billboard person on view.

Ochre-painted cedar, tiny boxed planet,
what else, what else?

Danger of mice, crawlies, varroa destructor
flattening a way through the streets of comb.

Must listen for
invaders.

9TH JUNE

All day they have dragged in
jewel-pins of nectar.

Now the whole of light rests.

12TH JUNE

Observe wet ground nettles have clogged with yellow roots,
flicker of water;
bee drinking,
knelt almost to lift from the trickle.

Nettles have grown into old men's bristles,
an endlessly rising Lazarus of bees.
This one bee is so newly built
it is almost impossible to give it time.

I watch its mechanism, its quartz pulse
drink bones of wetness from one of earth's holes.
Goes piloting up with added weight,
no doubt, its fuel-tank full.

Amazed at air's revolving energies. The sun:
each string of its hours is plucked and let slack.

14TH JUNE: SWARM?

What would you describe as commotion, friend
who watches from the window where the eyes
see the source of darkness,
and hear the shiver, fleck, and coiling twist,
a gutstring of bowed noise low down at home.

I did not quite expect that they would do this: go.

Examine,
almost crushing,
a thick slab of bees pouring out of the slot.

They went south . . .
False alarm. What next?

18TH JUNE: THE WORKS

Slow constant hum,
like a man will make when working
(or whistle).

Everything turning on duty in progression, as orderly;
touching and arcing points of weld.
Communication forms.

Long iron clouds,
because weather has importance, laws of conduct.
Stowing the world under rain
not yet heavy enough to fall.

The box is flooding with arrivals;
a weight measurable by thickenings of sound.

Experiment with this
in terms of how it's heard: up close, ear pressed
right to the jacket, shoulder-blade-thin panel back . . .

20TH JUNE: DUSTED BEES WITH ICING SUGAR (VARROA-PREVENTATIVE MEASURE)

With the hive tool prised the glued lid off;
slight cracking of propolis
(before I saw the citizens).
A sieve, a spoon; such words conjure baking.

This icing-sugar shower, this mad abrasive rev of wings
shaking the blizzard off with football stadium boos.
Grey ghost of bees,
of Pluto's.

Note, each bee grips with front legs
and flies the air across its thorax
on the spot.

13TH JULY

We checked. Bees have swarmed.

Nothing to say, except
we fed those left with syrup.

16TH JULY

The smaller bees are kittenish.
Tapped hive, the noise continues long.
Supposed to be a sign of health.
The drones are vast, bothersome.

25TH JULY: BROOD FRAME CHECK

12 Two thirds drawn comb on one side only.
1   Two sides drawn comb, a few cells filled.
3   Two sides drawn, 10% stores, queen cup broken open.
2   All drawn with 10% stores, no brood so far.
4   Drawn with some pollen, 10% stores, one empty
    queen cup, four bees feeding one bee with red tongues.
8   All drawn, some pollen, no brood.
5   All drawn, some pollen, no brood, surfeit of drones.
6   All drawn, some pollen, 10% stores, surfeit of drones.
7   30% drones, no stores, all drawn, one queen cup closed.
9   Not fully drawn, half to two thirds stores.
10 Drawn one side only, 10% stores.
11 Drawn one side, turned this around.

26TH JULY: IN THE GARDEN

I assume this creature is *my* bee.

There it is: one pulsing abdomen;
light brown, familiar, gently striped. Tongue
at drinking water.

Frail, how it concentrates
not solely for *itself.*
It makes one part.

What rhetoric the mind must be,
quite undisturbed.

Alas, how to read
mimesis;
not just reading what is ulterior,
ideal of a mother.

She needs water in this other mouth.
She
consists of minute projects,
like this alone.

How in her time
all co-exists,
not of itself.

27TH JULY

And is she in?

2ND AUGUST

Bees in irritated pieces;

touch is out of bounds.

                        One head
put to the side of what is inside.

Be very quiet,
harvesters have made their place, a row of four.
Just details these, but seem significant;
all exactly as *I* found it.

Dewy limbs just under an eave of zinc;
the rain is a sound against the hive.

My ear listens to an inside side.

12 One side part drawn.
 1 Both sides drawn, tiny proportion stores.
 3 Both sides stores, no queen cup present.
 2 Drawn, part stores.
 4 Drawn, stores, no queen cup present.
 5 Brood, capped and uncapped, white grubs. *Yes.*
 6 Brood, capped and uncapped, white grubs. *Yes, Yes.*
 7 Minute eggs, both sides. *Yes. Thanks.*
 8 Drawn and stores.
 9 Drawn and stores, some capped both sides.
10 Drawn and stores, both sides.
11 One side drawn only, turned.

First sign of new queen, mated and laying. *Alive.*

14TH AUGUST: BEE INSPECTOR

Today a DEFRA bee inspector clipped the wings of our queen.
What happened to those clippings?
Her flightless life is in that box of ours:
hoarded earth bit of her, no flight.

Nor will she collect her males into her mating flight
and fuck, and sever his genitals fiercely under the sun,
and creep back into darkness in that box again
she lays the eggs in for a lifetime's distance.

6TH SEPTEMBER: WILD COMB NOTES

I have the surprise comb in September's hive:
topped between frames, great pale construction
occluded, skinned and nibbled clean
bear's-skull of paper-white wax.

I hold a knife
and cut at the block of crystalline honeyed brain.

I taste its juice; sweet gods of the evergreen
woods' taste;
crushed music, bars and epiphanies of dripping air;
aggregated cells
of each and every flower's oddness there;

this sugar-map.

My tongue swarms like a fire has been lit
clean of its obstacles.
Right on its wet hearth-slab: solar heat.

I think, each bee's six heels
may be callipers for cell's wall angles.

12TH NOVEMBER: WINTER HONEY

To be honest, this is dark stuff; mud, tang
of bitter battery-tasting honey. The woods are in it.

Rot, decayed conglomerates, old garlic leaf, tongue
    wretched
by dead tastes, stubborn crystal, like rock. Ingredients:

ivy, sweat, testosterone, the blood of mites. Something
    human
in this flavour surely.

Has all the clamber, twist and grip
of light-starved roots, and beetle borehole dust.

Deciduous flare of dead leaf,
bright lights leached out like gypsum almost, alabaster
    ghost.

Do not think this unkind, the effect is slow
and salty in the mouth. A body's widow in her dying year.

It is bleak with taste and like meat, gamey.

This is the offal of the flowers' nectar.
The sleep of ancient insects runs on this.

Giant's Causeway hexagons we smeared on buttered toast
or just the pellets gouged straight from wax to mouth.

Try this addiction:
compounds of starched cold, lichen-grey light. What else seeps
    out?

Much work, one bee, ten thousand flowers a day
to make three teaspoons-worth of this
    disconcerting
    solid broth
of forest flora full of fox. Immune to wood shade now.

3RD DECEMBER: NOTES

Listen to the rain, the rain, the rain, like the wings and legs of bees
   walking across bees, like the lyre of a thought, a whole possible
   instrument of insects.
Listen to the rain, more rain, treadling earth to the sodden cold
   wet spun heads of this room, pacing the winter to and fro . . .

13TH DECEMBER: EVIDENCE OF COLD SNAP, A PAGE OF SCATTERED BEES FROM THE HIVE FLOOR

I torchlight through carrion;
the wooden effigy, cold-blood, crutch of one.

Here on this page, dour with weeks of stamped cold,
lie some twenty specimens.

Sodden in commune, grey with mould,
collapsed over hoops, distended structures.

A crouched patch of gut,
a crippled fur, crimped leg, ragged wing.

How to reactivate this mess?
No farmer could do it.

18TH DECEMBER

A transformer buzzes in the box, is tumbling on its core,
like winding the dark slowly over,
biding what it is, just conscious where-
abouts, a who? Without being there.

MIDWINTER

No bees venture.
Just one day's quiet after another's.

7TH JANUARY

Four inches of snow. The hive a hut
of silence and darkness.
I found a stick and scratched
a small translucent tunnel to the door.
Are you in there?
I've brought some light and air. No answer.

19TH JANUARY

Everything is senile.
I ask
   the box to
speak
   about
its bees.

14TH FEBRUARY: SONG

This beekeeper is bleak with lack
but he can heave a hunch up on his back;
he still can lift what needs begin a year,
and go out white from head to toe in gear,
under the blackbird's stark evocative
and murderous motor of keeping active,
since the hive is magnetic and grows magnetic . . .

Morning has streams of river sun,
cold stamping cold.

The bees are not out. Listen
to the grey rut of world,
the frozen track steams.

The bees are not out, listen.
I walked up close to the body of bees.

Just a door from this into their unlit state . . .
my mind sketches a congested bulk
in the cavity of the boards.

You have a manmade hut.
Do not shrug and go gloomy,
do not tip down your ball of
glued body parts.
The trick is life.

The bees are not out I muttered aloud.
But I just had my hands
rubbing their sticks of papery fingers,
I just had the nagging aeons, the quicksilver touch
of exposure getting me to keep still
to take its utter quiet of a picture.

The whole of the north is turning its screw into shatter.
The winter winds out.
How slow the Plough-memory of night dips and turns.

The bees are crouched in the door.
Quiet, I said, *listen*, I said.

They fan out of the door a Minerva beard,
lay out the flight paths, the locks of hair,
combing the air's amnesia to a noise.

28TH FEBRUARY

Do I dare to trust . . . these pets? They are not that.
Now as the rain skims down through rattled air
the last dead things, like skeletons of stones,
catch on my feet: *bee-friend*, the late dead things,
the skeleton of Christmas, fireworks of midnights vaporised,
the awkward purposeless haste of visitors . . .
These bees are visitors, how long they last, our guess.
The skeleton of song, the robin's cry note entering the bees.
Time very arthritic; the clock's joints ache.
Black bees, like models made of tar and grit, get stuck.
The queen inside them all; they, wall and bedding, cluster
walls' eyes, measuring and smelling, fitting . . .

1ST MARCH

Catkins.

7TH MARCH

Snowdrops.

12TH MARCH

The hive I opened today, bee friend, the comb empty.
Green lumps of mould strewn, the floor;
clogged dead understorey.

Morgue house it seems,
bees in their hundreds doomed out of time.

Some are just still living, operative. Are they in this
or do *they* mechanise just fractions of the consequence of living.

Autopsy, the worst atrocity of winter spell
has . . . under charge . . . famished guts,
a rotted lump of wreck.

Is your mind *dwindling*?
A conscious collective losing thought . . .
I thought, not you again.
New space for more to bring the sun in on the mouth.

Don't speak, it might use up presence. Why so weak?
What song is this which kills you singers as you sing it?
The cold is serious.

This is
our crematorium of hexagons, wild with crumbling debris;
crumbling
not so burnt as burnt-out, building *of* broken rooms.

Blown vaults, picked at with lean hands
gaunt from expenditure; creaky ticky bees
ransacked the last unforthcoming . . . opened cells:
Ivy honey too rock hard crystalline to extract.

(Advice: spray combs with water.)

What are the ends of winter-bees like then?
Brittle suitcases of fleeting trickery, empty.
I closed your box . . . Good luck.

General unburdening of wings, exclaims existence.
Our bees are not yet lit but stagger out
like gauze mantles for a gas light.

Pear tree changed to expressive.
Soon to explode crook-ends
from its thousand chins, knuckles, kneecaps, lids.

Touch: firm sprung leaf,
new horns of cattle, unpacking flower.
Touch: a crane yard of construction.
Almost seemed it would never happen.
I said almost seemed . . .

Now this roaring of boom-time, this action:
just a slip of the ancient.
The celandine remembers sun-winched paraphernalia.

You fly over.
You fly through . . . to the *other.*

(Right now an iron fleck creature
plays havoc with my writing hand;
it does not walk my trail of ink.

Observe the quivering body, legs scarce,
the head's pinprick.
This is I, it writes
in meandering sketch.

I blow it away
to a scrofulous bud . . .
glistening.)

The air sings white edges, *parts* of lichens . . .

20TH APRIL

Frost, and frost yesterday
and last night.

Strong little moon picked at your bones.

The pear on the brink
of unpacking its blossom.

One-bee marquees,
nectar festivities, tents.

One-day-only stalls of druggy sugars,
the beers of flowers.

Everything is dragged awake;
puts on its music clothes.

2ND MAY

The North Wind leans against your house
containing a mind of its own again;
its song, its bursts of breath are wilful cold reminders
of the dangerous airs.

Slowly you are tuning yourselves
into the small misheard scales, into a purpose.

A bee, a tine being struck was out:
sound like a rooting of thin flash
in liquid form poured from a bucket the size of an adult
tooth.
Magnet of listening, I to hear it
turned the pole of my head.

The hive door is there,
the landing board's grey slope of bleached wood.

One worker there,
banded as piano wire, freakish hands strumming.

Those *are* wings.
I was out, all my apertures very unfrightened.
Calm holes in my head heard the exact creak
of breaking nettles across the buzz.

23RD MAY

Silence please!

Glass air, glass furnace hit with a hammer. Sun
wildly lighting. Who is that smashing the walls?

If I extracted myself from the game
of being a keeper of danger,
the silent white suit which I wear
would unstuff itself, and hang
from the peg by the back door forever.

I would go naked, raw-boned, into that garden
if I extracted myself from this game of being keeper of bees.

I would go like a gaseous glass flesh
with a glassblower's mind
expanding over the very idea of my empty space.

1ST JUNE: HUM

Yesterday their tower-block of discrete units
was making new language out of cross-lapsed phrase.

No cease;
this madness is perpetual.
All works to a story fanning wildly
flames of plot outside the little door.

They must maintain the level of internal heat
to keep alive the characters they are.

Grip on and buzz;
emanation in the mad still air.
I am caused quietly
to hear.

These spy ears clamp
noise slowly gaining me
a radar bleep
in its circumference.

Looped with winding,
the armature of a motor, drifts of hum,
tone warp –
my mental notes cannot unknot.

25TH JUNE

Put seven frames into the Honey Super,
having taken the empty syrup feeder.

Unwearying winding of light high noise;

bees batting this pen and poem's paper.
Bee on my gloved hand,
heads of bees brushing over.

Small irritated power-tool shape of sound;

a spark of music, a score
going right down through my head;
a sheet of music
grinding the halves of my brain apart.

I am two beekeepers, just in phase:
two suns, two fields of air,
two lapsing horizons, superimposed.

5TH JULY: BUSINESS OF FRAMES

The hive needs frames
or brace comb fills the space.
So I make frames: I learn the work
of making batches up from pre-fab kits.

My concentration collects to beekeeper dew-point
demanding the kitchen, all of its table.

Knock tenon to mortice,
Who's there?
The foundation, a sheet of stamped-out coda.

Note, each mutating shadow of a tack
creeps to its nailhead . . .

. . . 12 frames are stacked.

6TH JULY: BRACE COMB

Part of the moon bees have
was found in flowers:

the unseen stance, the quality of things
in human palm-sized pieces;

a vital organ of two days' deep work
growing a topography of common;
the wicks of eggs,
new and clipped.

I twist the brace comb off
and brush the bodies
of bees alone;
legs hooked in their world hang.

The rusks of hexagon
are mute strength in volume;

plain as a Shaker would fashion a drawer;
materially earnest,
divine, pure of toil.

16TH JULY

Agitated,
you opened the hive under a great parasol
to keep the hive rain-free;
shaking of workers into air.

And there were the frames,
fat wads of untasted honey
now and *here*: animal, particular weight.

Bees, tail-raised scorpions of moment.
Scores of drones,
the heart of drone time.
Beware: increasing roar.

Stabbed!

Three stings to the right hand.
You, one to the neck.

Witches of black poison went screeching
figures of eight,
all broomstick and flight path.

Black poison throbbed.
My rivers wretched, staggering at undertow,
gripped my feet.

And you, agitated, no sight of the queen,
whispered, as if in a calm state, *Are you there?*

Two queen cups, stored, like closed kegs of brew.

17TH JULY: KILLING DRONES

Today cut comb with drone cells from the lower frame.
Too many drones,
one tenth of all here this month;
they eat the stores.

Capped brood in ancient pots.
(Suspect no queen present,
she with clipped wings, gone.)
Respect the unborn dead.

Hatched heads waggle, *they* are trapped;
they understand
the pageant of the mating flight will come.
And yet not born yet, these fated.

Two queen cells ripen fat with burden;
evolve same plan.
(Winding sound increased.)
Which queen will wake first?

This game we hold and do not possess but use.
This farm is cities;
good health;
wing sheen like threshold stones.

Kneel eyes;
note, no graffiti of foul brood or mould;
comb dark with capped brood *is* pixels.
Wings good, not ragged; the honey clear,
will not take yet.

Took one board of comb with hatching drones;
heads chewing out their caps.
Threw the buoyant, tarry, dark wax into the river.
Barge of ballast: heads a trout may seize.

Slow flows, away it goes,
twelve-headed river-hearse of the emergent.

No flame for them.

23RD JULY: NOISE & WASTE

Today the hive
is trying out *its* harmonics,

a weepy low fugue I think to burning sun.
The loss of flowers is overwhelming:

dry sheaths and packets
stapled onto brown skulls.

The nagging air swings gibbets of drought.
Some clumps of the world are barred.
The dump stinks in flowerbeds, weedbeds,
and the river's clogged two miles of hemlock rots.

Mangled carapaces fall out of air
skinny in their little traps of make-up.

A chimera of scrap parts.
Grass-blade emerald twisted.
Glitter paste of bumps & grazes.
The air's ears are traumatised,

and on the flames of the hour
just a whiff of decline,
just a whiff more.

The white dry heat jangles;
it's like a kiln is shaking at the corners.

Tomorrow,
must search the dawn's damp ash
for broken mirrors.

29TH JULY: LATE AFTERNOON

Bees in other hives out there are dying in droves.

Now,
now,
and now,

the wind drags bleakly, other horizons paw
at our premise, edge, dregs of far points,

anemophilous noise
which shifts and lifts a tambourine
of black, black news.

Tree-flapping, guitar-like,
string-scrape signatures;
the wind's bee chanting scores,
potential, potential collapses.

This is an uncertain, uncertain tragic time of *ours*:
Rocks in the field, like *old* stone hives.

29TH JULY: INTERIOR

My bed here, say four hundred yards south-east of the hive,
my bed here.

Awake in the zoo-dead-of-night
I listen in on the cages of the day's hours.

There is that question,
trapped and circling a hole in the floor.
A slurry of collapsed swarm agitates in there,

like the very black bowl of a
dead stare into itching solid.

And there in that bludgeoned hole is the idea of a calf,
not broken, but fully bruised, and blocked up with clay plugs.

Mistaken bees blackly weep from its ears.

The colony has one time: it's like a gas
dispersing towards the lowest of pressures.

7TH AUGUST: PROPERTY

A frame of honeycomb is in the kitchen:
just a candle, vigil, out of respect.
It's like a body I visit
laid on the table's midnight.

The smell is first; under its pinewood resin
the smell of light is in a miracle:
I – criminal – touch

its tear-easy skin of skeletal reef.
(Best use of space for minimal effort.)
No waste for them, just work,
and days of nectar flow are nearing end.

Flowers are here, springs of them,
wells and weightless drops of briefest sex;
a wax shroud turned down at its corners;
a dead skin most beautifully scented,
drawn out of dark.

When touched,
observe the way
that light swells in the crack
and golden-eyes.

But it is cold,
I paid for it with hooks across my flesh.

25TH AUGUST: AFTERMATH

columbine   pea   dead nettle

foxglove   tansy   hemp agrimony

　　herb Robert   Sedum
                                    Welsh poppy

meadowsweet   St John's wort
                     thistle

27TH AUGUST

The spider's season opens,
rat tooth-marks begin to appear;

almost just a tempering of vision.

So in a coat
I go up to the ochre house of you in there.

How bees touch and re-align their touch.

Light in migration;
noise of a body in continual repair . . .

29TH SEPTEMBER

Archangel sunlight
held to a flower's remnant,
a weighing of balance in the sway of asters
I saw two days before,

as though the angled plane
of the flat face of September's sun
had made each flower's inflorescence
mirror its gift.

We are inflected:
note, bees give by this.

7TH OCTOBER: WASPS

Torrents of wasp — five at once, fifty, erratic, persistent.
Bee peace is bombed at this house, but
distortion in their world *is* articulate.

The air's single cell is clear as a bauble, and delicate.
They know the invertebrate bubble of the planet's life-jacket
and do sustain it — this weird filigree of livid minute.

It seems mirage to us, sceptical ill-tuned folk;
bees heatwave off the hive's wooden mouth.

As for wasps, it's like
short sparks which jump from loose plug leads
into an engine's block.

Today then, I watched a threading of loose ends.

11TH OCTOBER: MICHAELMAS DAISIES

Bright day, afternoon, no precise time,
the hour-light at sunlight's maximum.
Michaelmas daisies are set to now.

Alight honey bee, I do feel
the extremity of your spectrum
that homes on an unsteady cymbal of flower's radial.
I heard it shivering tissh as you touched on its platform;
a close-up protracting of tongue suck in a zip-noise;
a faint sweet wet from a nectary's spring.

We observe the yellowness of dying leaves:
it's like gates, it's like precincts being drawn
to 3D's infinity point of perspective.

The shawl-work of summer has grown unwoven,
tuned into a brittle, rottable music of roughage and stubborn dregs.

The earth-she wanders, going blind and odd,
like air, pushing a trolley full of dead flowers;

is that not you, Persephone, or Eurydice, or just a likeness
creeping?

Listen,
small pitch patch of bee-wing song
is strung with a sound made of now's last flowerheads.

Maybe just
our time ticks because we have a time to accord to;
and all the machinery is lifted by briefest experience.

Echoes are something more quiet
than a world's bee paused on a ledge at an edge

for a life of a few weeks
cycling up from millennia's blackness.

(We are played in your existence;
the Shadows we bring
fall just a note's breadth
off your heart-rate's strumming.)

16TH OCTOBER: SUPER CHECK

Removed the Honey Super.
No stores,
just a dry, papery wax-comb of empties.
No sugar syrup touched;
what is wrong with supplements?

Stand mesmerised
at this landing board.
It is familiar, all-relevant –
a collateral winding of wire-string song.

Think what paths would be
if *we* could envisage
flights tracked to their nectaries'
pin-point co-ordinates.

A round dance tells trails
in mid-air's mile or so round-trip.

We bring, bee friend, yellow pollen on our legs.

In human terms, it seems OK.
Your bright sharp blackthorn-rickety bodies pass each way.

I lay a minute's judgement:
minute, small, perhaps a touch vacant,
a field-slack lethargy, something I dreamt
still nameless, coagulating its weak-spot under our nose.

Burdock burrs gather and catch on our gauze
as we hack

the thicket clear of the hive
for winter air to not stagnate.

We suffer damp, dear neighbour – you should not.

17TH OCTOBER: AUDIO RECORDING

Today, lifted the hive's in-winding with our gloved hands,
set up microphones to amplify, and catch
and keep and zoom in on your snatch
of fieldsound din;
what makes your orchestration, dialect, anima: in.

You are studding our vestments.

Tonight,
I transcribed each track to a score,
a foley for winter-prayer to repeat
a river wound onto spools of tape-like time
like bolts of fallen light you whisper in sine-
wave. And I play back
to will alive your hyper-thyroid slurred to human slack.

At queen's depth,
you were fast-forwarding a stress;
this is your speed of conversation;
just a fizzing spaghetti-
junction of swerves
over your sanctuary's inner sanctum.

How privileged we are to lower ears in
and slow to one wingbeat-per-second,
go between headphones into deep stereo.

I have your hive's unique vertigo

at 24 bit, 48 mega hertz,
digital, precise, approximate.

Black honey in its dark brood cells
is a wild liquor of ecstatic work.
Bright sun and gauze exhaust its details.

We fall to our second winter, bees.
The grass flaked out of frost white bones last night,
emaciatingly bright.

Your ultra-commune is still unlocked, you fly,
but feel the globe of cluster remembered
like vapour ghost breath smoke-ring trick of circular,
contracted.

And we, beekeepers,
can only open the book part way to read what is unsaid.
Not being your drones we do not see like you.

Eyes fed and lit up.
Eyes starved and kicked out.
That was a drone's life, all summer's sight.

We lean on our human eyes,
absorbed into honey black with cocoon stain.

28TH NOVEMBER: MUMMIFIED FLOWERS

Day-of-the-dead twenty-six days late.
Black star of cow parsley is fate
in cellulose; black hand bone of meadowsweet
a fountain's ruin; and underground, live root and antiseptic.

We dead-of-insects keep one crane fly in the house,
dead family ghost invertebrate –
I learn to love its structures.

In your bee-garden, tethers slacken;
it is all ribs and crucifixion-
styled event
in slippery brown black;
the black of winter trout,
for example, leaps to mind.

But it is plants whose flower you sucked I study:
now pharaohs bound in corpses of stiff earth;
their embalming is theirs.
Frog faces made vague of body.
St John's wort stands unzipping one side.
Yarrow, charred twig in dry mouth.

I could go on in this crypt voice;
the vault is a museum for muses.

I look over flower-beds, catacombs, tilted spear leaf,
amphorae of dusts.

One preserved canoe oar's decrepit end
of what a flower needed to get over;
sandal-made footprints of remain,
frozen effigy of airs.

The biology is lessons in death.

I snap a pipe of hemp agrimony off.
Its ice is un-scrolled papyrus,
a very old hieroglyph for 'dead light'.

Two black leg-stumps stick up where the earth
walked a plant up. I swear
it was there
carrying a gourd of honey in its hair.

6TH DECEMBER: HIVE CHECK

Checked hive,
removed base-board at noon,
hoping to dry
the damp air soon.

Fiddled out dead wings
from the mesh,
journal of a bee's head,
particular bits

of a knee fell down,
sting, tongue,
dropped from the grille,
but these dead bees are insulation.

Looked to the south:
a moist flood-lamp heaviness of sun's
frost shape.

The hive black with damp,
bogged in burial, mouldy bedding.

It's hunger you grow,
keeping a queen light in your dream sight.
She at the tip of the pyramid of your hierarchy
but it's different.

Outside, broadly, gingerbread dusklight;
a granular snowfall litters woods.

I slide the board back in, close you up.

We haunt our bees with tiny regular checks.
The board below the hive exhibits mites,
it is quite clear
a change has altered us and arrangements.

The parasitic present is in chains.
Home: sudden prison.

Black as grit stare of particulate;
moody revealing of a plague;
destructive, irreversibly inlaid
into this cedar-box of drag.

Pinholes in the day's air, the plummet breathless:
I wheel still, bend my gauzed eyes,
blind in the mystery
of its onboard navigator, assessing parasite.

Appendages:
those mites make apertures and drink out bee,
the hole stays open for this beverage:
copper blood.

I have rehearsed the snag.
Now it is real weight, life's ferment, quiet it is.

The mite-count reveals eighteen:
crab-legged, as described in books,
flat button-shell.
I grow words I would spit:
oxide black, vitreous as slag.
Day biting, and the North's trees hiss,
and the North's wind's catastrophic noise
is stiff toes tripping over stones of a problem.

Curse
the arched cloud-fretted sky
that brought this, blows with sickness.

Rush to the house, and make enquiries.
The whole indoors is bent with disaster.
Phone down: I've sent for medicine.

18TH DECEMBER: SNOW AND
INTERVENTION

Unscrew the cap, invert and squeeze
this bottle between frames into bee-gap.

(Water, saccharose, citric, oxalic, formic acids
& propolis extract,
diverse, unspecified, essential oils of what?)

A stagger of waiting
leans over the hour's clock-hand's seconds.
Jutting harp strings of light,
ligaments of noise take flight.

It's like a head being tapped out:
the weaker bees mass and fan at the door's ledge,
become a gangplank of intent to leave.
They slow-wing to the snow-floor.

The blackbirds are interested,
landing an assembly to constrict this unfortunate rink.

For an hour of daylight
the hive clears out the bric-a-brac of infested.

Before I go, I smear thin belts of their own honey back
along brood-frame bars.
Hangs of it plumb into the dark.

How did it go, this song of chemistry?
It's like a dream it should not be so,
bees misjudging the gaunt-of-heat world.

A hundred bees dead at a touch – that is not much
of thousands in a box,
but, black on the snow they go,
dropped bag of dead luck.

We do observe your plight – We, and the blackbird
in our danger. Observe – merely, yes.

21ST DECEMBER: SOLSTICE FOR BEES

The sun leans at its annual alignment:
bare day and short,
the sky bleached and chattering with a slight adjustment.

Light's skeleton puts back its fingers and flicks
the spectral end constant,
and bees just switch the wires of their song opposite;
winding the same sound the other way up.

Like hanks of yarn, this endurance of eavesdrop
grows wound and looped, and invariably it twists
between the wings and the ear.

May you come back
through the hole in the world's syllable.

4TH JANUARY: THE HONEY JAR

I do not take the honey but lift it down:
the jar of it on the high shelf
is a ghost of goings-on,
a kept world-part of their summer,
and having it is prying on wood hedge, forest floor.

I have the whole life coat of light passed through it,
hanging by the tail over the table edge.
It is smeared with flame.
I have to drag up flame by the face
and cradle it like candlelight,
and it stares me out of my wits in this gloomy
month's crisis.
You, honey, pervade this place.
Its gatherers are on ritual guard through rites of famine.
Poverty becomes bones,
bones fingers, fingers loose, and loose the showman
on the stage of its miracle –
I cannot forget that word's
attempting arc over all silence.
Miracle, another word for this,
opens gold gates: a paraphrase for survival.

Off-key is a slow angel of returning cellulose;
its sugars breed blindly underground.
All of snowlight's heartbroken month is scratchy
and cut back to a diagram for pruning.

Requirement: for the legacy to work.
Requirement: for the wild tendency
of light to return on its wheel of the nights
the bare sun;

      out of its ephitaphion
to call up the signature ghosts of green limb.

It is lavish with cold, it is almost insane.
Bees, in your wax insulation,
some of you sleep the raw, leftover, virtuoso
of you all; it diminishes daily.

6TH JANUARY: EPIPHANY

Each day's length's procession is hummed barefoot.
Like martyrs, some roll the road's infinity over frosty thorns.

May you carry your mother-queen to the year's haven,
at 1500 eggs-per-day speed.

13TH JANUARY: FALSE SPRING

Week's long hoax of mild weather
and bees wander like fools.

Up in the woods' hedge, catkins are no hope,
not yet let down smeared with yellow.

And only points of shoots are protracted – hand against hand,
finger to finger – and no crocus flower's first food, no protein.

Beekeepers are despairing on the telephone,
dream of cloches on the springtime floor.

Helios is given bonfires by some.

15TH JANUARY: HERB TEA

I read of a herb tea for bees
in which nettle, chamomile act as the basis.
It fortifies the problem of keeping bees,
but that is the problem: keeping.

I read of exchanges,
i.e. a formic acid in the nettle.

Bees bring this trace
and net it through the wild we call our garden,
as they work it.
Formic acid for nectar, pollination: this is trade.

I go to the sanctuary kitchen to make the tea,
add grains of salt and their own honey (10%) to boiling water.
(Be warned: imported honeys most likely
contain the nosema or foul brood spores.)

It cools to stone-heat on the side.

Liquor to set on the crown-board of the box
now winding steam abracadabras, plant oils
wetted to aroma;
the steel saucepan turned ancient.

And then, like a car mechanic, opened and closed the hive's bonnet,
turned back over the chewy clay in deep footfall without the brew.

24TH/25TH JANUARY: BEES DIE

29TH JANUARY: APOLLO MOUSE

Suddenly the house is dishevelled;
all in the sixth sense way of things,
a gaunt, empty, weight of bereavement.

A tramp mouse moves in; we know by excrement:
an Apollo from cold stone and bitter hunger.

Still, it is the coldest winter on record.
So much has changed in the way of house-keeping:
wax bitten shreds of body and furniture.

A dust-coating thickens to a taste's spectre,
and the quiet lack of bees is weighty.

The quartz honey upstairs is tampered loose.
You could not eat what was painstakingly gathered.

But it's like a hearthstone, a house,
for earwig and weather finding its door open.
Three days and squatters are regular,
infest the house; each as vagrant as any dweller.

Your trace is treasure,
despite the house mouse and dirt.

2ND FEBRUARY: PROOF

I go to the shelf where the honey lives,
and say, this is testament: bees did exist.

10TH FEBRUARY:
DISMANTLING THE COMB

Morning drizzle at ten a.m.
We open the hive, bee friend, last time
& it's like entering Pompeii,
much like that gritty, accumulating, reduction
in voice you get in shock;
for a minute we just hang up our arms
with frames of comb and stop.

Look, they are just where they were.
I did not expect to see a bee's point of death
like a chink in a protractor's half circumference;
sky perfect on wings, a storm-paddle sun like a torch left on
in a dead woman's hand.

We lift comb after comb only to find segments
of the cluster,
a sliced globe of clinked and magnetic sister.
And the queen, there:

intermission.

The room's sarcophagus of waft
ripe with not-quite embalmed must and antiseptic strange resin
staining our lungs and skin,
frames of beekeeper's mind.

There's an illness and beauty of detritus.
Our hands touch to face, finger, lip;
tongue takes smears of the gagging, like pollen of taste.

A slow word racks between our ears, once,
to conclude the problem: 'Dead'.

I run back for bin bags to take off the comb,
to burn the brood nest, to bag and to burn.

Keep two frames, friend, to observe, choose, loosen, lift
the very centre of the cluster right here
onto the kitchen table, under the light.

I rub one finger across stopped bees.
They in their cells headfirst, did they just stop there?
Soft as iron filings, grown lifted, quilted
with magnet.

A troubling soft streak –
they should rise and attack, but no instinct,
no quirk of uprising, only lack of resistance.

Our day has shrunk to the atrocity: brood-nest's
black pots, empty shops, eye sockets, pockets,
the perfected model of a fatal act.

Something else will re-invent it –
moths, mice, lice will eat it.

I torch into cells – eyes fit and focus-pull
in descent – to the fairytale's well.
It's like the grain of a moon, a spoon-back of pale no one,
just the pail of an egg's dry opal empty of hunger.

Every pit has a rice grain in it.
This is our prognosis: starved house.
She was laying in a warm spell, she was deluded
by a freak of the mild, unreal spring,
hazels just days off manufacturing
their dreadlocks of pollen;
how close she was, how close.

Stare, friend, an end, bees still in cells,
preserved shut-winged, fluttering by breath – that's death,
like stuck in strobelight.

Crusty oxide: describe the sealing cap
part-chewed like a split boil,
the white wet wax sheen of a grub not yet shrunken.
On the threads of our apiarist's eyes
we dangle into the nursery, count, re-count
roughly forty new eggs, died dividing their cells.

We house in our hands the corpse of a city:
cell-ends, dog-ends,
smells of apple, Germolene, urea.
We bag up thousands: foresters, workers,
dismal in drizzle.

10TH FEBRUARY: QUEEN

I keep the queen, she is long in my hand,
her legs slightly pliant;
folded, dropped down, wings flat
that flew her mating flight
to the sun and back, full of spermatozoa, dronesong.
She was made mechanically ecstatic.
I magnify what she is, magnify her skews and centres.
How downy she is, fur like a fox's greyness, like a thistle's mane.
Wings perfect, abdomen subtle in shades of brittle;
her rear legs are big in the lens;
feet like hung anchors are hooks for staying on cell-rims.
Veins in her wings are a rootwork of rivers,
all echo and interlace. This is her face, compound eye.
I look at the slope of her head, the mouth's proboscis;
her thin tongue piercing is pink as cut flesh, flash glass.
Some hairs feather and split below the head.
Those eyes are like castanets, cast nets;
woman all feral and ironwork, I slip
under the framework, into the subtle.
The wing is jointed at the black leather shoulder.
I wear it, I am soft to stroke, the lower blade fans.
Third generation queen of our stock,
you fall as I turn. I hold your hunchback;
a carcase of lightness, no grief, part animal, part flower.

3RD JULY: GIFT

A noise is on the loose, today;
black winding pendulum weight of core
by the main road to Radstock.
I take a saw to cut down the bough of a swarm.

The air's innards have sprung apart.
I am netted in trawls of strumming bee.
Can I say
what kind of halo absorbs me?

In and in and in a morass, fast place, race,
roadside and twenty years of brittle bramble
thick with bees,
thorns snagging my beekeeper's costume.

I did not expect a calm lack of resistance like this.
Not one sting as I handle fizzing thousands,

entering the physiology of a heatwave;
their aspect, divine as electrons;
physically deranged sound
like a fool holding its freedom.

You *are* winged strange kind, you are nerval.
Inside your fluency,
mirrors facing all mirrors shade back to eternity.

Standing in the middle of your intellect:
must catch and keep.
My shroud conceals a skeleton of tensions, not me; I'm right out
in the open livid whirlwind of metropolis rid of its rooms.

I bring this hive,
Come in.

Bees from hands drop slowly as honey.
I close the lid on them, I wish the willing in.

Bring in a sound like Hestia, like hearth, like heart.

And they convey
the queen flame through the door.
I'd swear
you are descendants of the dead that swarmed last year
from here;
the width of your banding, that particular
taper of abdomen, colour . . .

I leave the box to gain its anima.

Now, darkfall, I return to claim.
Detect
new-trying gritty clicky voice of thousands;
a chord of assembly tuning its domestic.
(Note, each colony different,
an amicable pitch inside all else.)

I listen
to the insular, poached wild body under the bonnet.

Finder, keeper. Life's instrument.

This in my arms (this heavy box) I take to the apiary.
I look at the road we have to cross.
You are not fully ordinary, bees.
The ordinary mortals go by in cars.

ACKNOWLEDGEMENTS

Acknowledgements are due to the editors of *Blaze Vox*, *Granta*, *London Review of Books*, *Poetry Ireland Review*, *Poetry Review*, *The Rialto*, and the organisers of the Bridport Prize. A few bee poems appeared as a pamphlet, *Pages from Bee Journal* (Isinglass).

Grateful thanks to Chris Lewis-Smith who keeps the bees with me, Alan Weaver for explaining over the telephone how to catch a swarm, and Julian Willford for supplying our first colony.

I am indebted to Jane Borodale, Derek Southall, Jon Hill, Valerie Hill, Annie Hunt, Sam Hunt, David Beatty, Kitty Aldridge, Robin Robertson, Peter Straus and Carol Ann Duffy.